MW00341523

CONTENTS: STRAN

Whole Numbers: Division

Name _____   Date _____

Whole Numbers: Division

1. $9\overline{)36}$ 2. $6\overline{)84}$ 3. $7\overline{)259}$ 4. $5\overline{)2,795}$

5. $32\overline{)6,272}$ 6. $23\overline{)6,330}$ 7. $296\overline{)110,363}$

Write the remainder as a fraction.

8. $273\overline{)6,848}$

Write the answer in decimal form.
Round to the nearest hundredth.

9. $73\overline{)8,132}$

Name _____   Date _____

Whole Numbers: Division

REMEMBER?

$5\overline{)15}$

||||| ||||| |||||

A

1. $12 \div 2 =$ _____   **2.** $4 \div 2 =$ _____

3. $14 \div 2 =$ _____   **4.** $18 \div 2 =$ _____

5. $18 \div 3 =$ _____   **6.** $6 \div 3 =$ _____

7. $15 \div 3 =$ _____   **8.** $30 \div 3 =$ _____   **9.** $16 \div 2 =$ _____

10. $10 \div 2 =$ _____   **11.** $24 \div 3 =$ _____   **12.** $3 \div 3 =$ _____

13. $12 \div 3 =$ _____   **14.** $21 \div 3 =$ _____   **15.** $27 \div 3 =$ _____

16. $6 \div 2 =$ _____   **17.** $2 \div 2 =$ _____   **18.** $20 \div 2 =$ _____

- -

B

1. $2\overline{)12}$ **2.** $2\overline{)6}$ **3.** $2\overline{)18}$ **4.** $2\overline{)2}$ **5.** $2\overline{)4}$

6. $3\overline{)24}$ **7.** $3\overline{)3}$ **8.** $3\overline{)30}$ **9.** $3\overline{)21}$ **10.** $3\overline{)27}$

11. $3\overline{)12}$ **12.** $3\overline{)9}$ **13.** $3\overline{)18}$ **14.** $2\overline{)8}$ **15.** $2\overline{)20}$

16. $2\overline{)14}$ **17.** $2\overline{)16}$ **18.** $2\overline{)10}$ **19.** $3\overline{)6}$ **20.** $3\overline{)15}$

Name _____   Date _____

Whole Numbers: Division

REMEMBER?
$4\overline{)20}$
‖‖‖ ‖‖‖ ‖‖‖ ‖‖‖ ‖‖‖

A

1. $4\overline{)4}$ 2. $4\overline{)8}$ 3. $4\overline{)16}$ 4. $4\overline{)28}$

5. $5\overline{)15}$ 6. $5\overline{)5}$ 7. $5\overline{)35}$ 8. $5\overline{)10}$

9. $4\overline{)12}$ 10. $4\overline{)24}$ 11. $4\overline{)32}$ 12. $5\overline{)45}$ 13. $5\overline{)40}$

14. $5\overline{)30}$ 15. $5\overline{)20}$ 16. $4\overline{)36}$ 17. $4\overline{)40}$ 18. $5\overline{)25}$

- -

B

1. $28 \div 4 =$ ____   2. $32 \div 4 =$ ____   3. $24 \div 4 =$ ____

4. $20 \div 4 =$ ____   5. $4 \div 4 =$ ____   6. $30 \div 5 =$ ____

7. $45 \div 5 =$ ____   8. $40 \div 5 =$ ____   9. $5 \div 5 =$ ____

10. $10 \div 5 =$ ____   11. $35 \div 5 =$ ____   12. $25 \div 5 =$ ____

13. $8 \div 4 =$ ____   14. $16 \div 4 =$ ____   15. $28 \div 4 =$ ____

16. $12 \div 4 =$ ____   17. $15 \div 5 =$ ____   18. $20 \div 5 =$ ____

19. $40 \div 4 =$ ____   20. $50 \div 5 =$ ____   21. $27 \div 9 =$ ____

Whole Numbers: Division

REMEMBER?

$$6 \overline{)\,18}$$

|||||| |||||| ||||||

A

1. $48 \div 6 =$ ____

2. $6 \overline{)\,48}$

3. $24 \div 6 =$ ____

4. $6 \overline{)\,24}$

5. $36 \div 6 =$ ____

6. $6 \overline{)\,36}$

7. $12 \div 6 =$ ____

8. $6 \overline{)\,12}$

9. $42 \div 6 =$ ____

10. $6 \overline{)\,42}$

11. $63 \div 7 =$ ____

12. $7 \overline{)\,63}$

13. $6 \div 6 =$ ____

14. $6 \overline{)\,6}$

15. $56 \div 7 =$ ____

16. $7 \overline{)\,56}$

17. $42 \div 7 =$ ____

18. $7 \overline{)\,42}$

B

1. $14 \div 7 =$ ____

2. $7 \overline{)\,14}$

3. $60 \div 6 =$ ____

4. $6 \overline{)\,60}$

5. $21 \div 7 =$ ____

6. $7 \overline{)\,21}$

7. $35 \div 7 =$ ____

8. $7 \overline{)\,35}$

9. $54 \div 6 =$ ____

10. $6 \overline{)\,54}$

11. $70 \div 7 =$ ____

12. $7 \overline{)\,70}$

13. $49 \div 7 =$ ____

14. $7 \overline{)\,49}$

15. $28 \div 7 =$ ____

16. $7 \overline{)\,28}$

17. $18 \div 6 =$ ____

18. $6 \overline{)\,18}$

19. $30 \div 6 =$ ____

20. $6 \overline{)\,30}$

Whole Numbers: Division

A

1. $8 \overline{)80}$ **2.** $80 \div 8 =$ ____   **3.** $8 \overline{)16}$ **4.** $16 \div 8 =$ ____

5. $8 \overline{)32}$ **6.** $32 \div 8 =$ ____   **7.** $8 \overline{)40}$ **8.** $40 \div 8 =$ ____

9. $8 \overline{)48}$ **10.** $48 \div 8 =$ ____   **11.** $9 \overline{)81}$ **12.** $81 \div 9 =$ ____

13. $9 \overline{)54}$ **14.** $54 \div 9 =$ ____   **15.** $9 \overline{)45}$ **16.** $45 \div 9 =$ ____

17. $9 \overline{)27}$ **18.** $27 \div 9 =$ ____   **19.** $8 \overline{)72}$ **20.** $72 \div 8 =$ ____

B

1. $8 \overline{)64}$ **2.** $64 \div 8 =$ ____   **3.** $8 \overline{)56}$ **4.** $56 \div 8 =$ ____

5. $9 \overline{)90}$ **6.** $90 \div 9 =$ ____   **7.** $9 \overline{)9}$ **8.** $9 \div 9 =$ ____

9. $9 \overline{)72}$ **10.** $72 \div 9 =$ ____   **11.** $9 \overline{)36}$ **12.** $36 \div 9 =$ ____

13. $9 \overline{)18}$ **14.** $18 \div 9 =$ ____   **15.** $8 \overline{)24}$ **16.** $24 \div 8 =$ ____

17. $8 \overline{)8}$ **18.** $8 \div 8 =$ ____   **19.** $9 \overline{)63}$ **20.** $63 \div 9 =$ ____

Whole Numbers: Division

1. $5\overline{)50}$ 2. $8\overline{)80}$ 3. $8\overline{)72}$ 4. $8\overline{)64}$ 5. $9\overline{)90}$

6. $1\overline{)1}$ 7. $3\overline{)18}$ 8. $3\overline{)27}$ 9. $3\overline{)3}$ 10. $8\overline{)56}$

11. $6\overline{)0}$ 12. $5\overline{)40}$ 13. $3\overline{)12}$ 14. $9\overline{)72}$ 15. $8\overline{)48}$

16. $2\overline{)18}$ 17. $1\overline{)3}$ 18. $3\overline{)9}$ 19. $7\overline{)35}$ 20. $8\overline{)40}$

21. $4\overline{)4}$ 22. $6\overline{)18}$ 23. $9\overline{)54}$ 24. $7\overline{)28}$ 25. $8\overline{)32}$

26. $4\overline{)40}$ 27. $2\overline{)14}$ 28. $1\overline{)5}$ 29. $7\overline{)21}$ 30. $5\overline{)0}$

31. $4\overline{)36}$ 32. $9\overline{)36}$ 33. $6\overline{)24}$ 34. $5\overline{)25}$ 35. $5\overline{)5}$

36. $7\overline{)35}$ 37. $2\overline{)0}$ 38. $6\overline{)60}$ 39. $1\overline{)7}$ 40. $5\overline{)10}$

41. $9\overline{)18}$ 42. $4\overline{)16}$ 43. $2\overline{)8}$ 44. $6\overline{)36}$ 45. $5\overline{)15}$

46. $7\overline{)56}$ 47. $4\overline{)24}$ 48. $2\overline{)4}$ 49. $6\overline{)48}$ 50. $1\overline{)9}$

Whole Numbers: Division

1. $5 \overline{)50}$ 2. $2 \overline{)20}$ 3. $7 \overline{)70}$ 4. $4 \overline{)40}$ 5. $3 \overline{)18}$

6. $6 \overline{)60}$ 7. $2 \overline{)18}$ 8. $7 \overline{)63}$ 9. $4 \overline{)36}$ 10. $7 \overline{)7}$

11. $1 \overline{)10}$ 12. $5 \overline{)40}$ 13. $9 \overline{)27}$ 14. $3 \overline{)3}$ 15. $7 \overline{)0}$

16. $8 \overline{)80}$ 17. $6 \overline{)48}$ 18. $2 \overline{)14}$ 19. $7 \overline{)49}$ 20. $7 \overline{)21}$

21. $4 \overline{)4}$ 22. $1 \overline{)8}$ 23. $5 \overline{)0}$ 24. $9 \overline{)45}$ 25. $7 \overline{)28}$

26. $3 \overline{)24}$ 27. $8 \overline{)64}$ 28. $6 \overline{)36}$ 29. $2 \overline{)10}$ 30. $7 \overline{)35}$

31. $7 \overline{)14}$ 32. $4 \overline{)12}$ 33. $1 \overline{)6}$ 34. $5 \overline{)20}$ 35. $9 \overline{)0}$

36. $5 \overline{)30}$ 37. $4 \overline{)16}$ 38. $8 \overline{)48}$ 39. $6 \overline{)24}$ 40. $2 \overline{)6}$

41. $1 \overline{)3}$ 42. $4 \overline{)20}$ 43. $8 \overline{)0}$ 44. $1 \overline{)4}$ 45. $5 \overline{)10}$

46. $8 \overline{)40}$ 47. $4 \overline{)0}$ 48. $8 \overline{)24}$ 49. $1 \overline{)2}$ 50. $6 \overline{)12}$

Whole Numbers: Division

REMEMBER?
$\begin{array}{r} 1 \leftarrow 1 \\ 2\overline{)24} \times 2 \\ -2\downarrow \leftarrow 2 \end{array}$

A

1. $3\overline{)39}$ 2. $2\overline{)42}$ 3. $4\overline{)48}$ 4. $2\overline{)26}$

5. $2\overline{)46}$ 6. $5\overline{)55}$ 7. $4\overline{)84}$ 8. $2\overline{)62}$

9. $4\overline{)88}$ 10. $2\overline{)64}$ 11. $3\overline{)66}$ 12. $3\overline{)96}$ 13. $2\overline{)86}$

B

1. $2\overline{)22}$ 2. $3\overline{)36}$ 3. $2\overline{)28}$ 4. $4\overline{)44}$ 5. $2\overline{)44}$

6. $3\overline{)63}$ 7. $5\overline{)55}$ 8. $4\overline{)48}$ 9. $2\overline{)48}$ 10. $3\overline{)39}$

11. $2\overline{)64}$ 12. $4\overline{)84}$ 13. $2\overline{)82}$ 14. $4\overline{)88}$ 15. $3\overline{)99}$

Whole Numbers: Division

REMEMBER?

$$1 \leftarrow 1$$
$$4\overline{)52} \quad \times 4$$
$$\underline{-4\downarrow} \leftarrow 4$$
$$1$$

A

1. $5\overline{)75}$ 2. $4\overline{)64}$ 3. $6\overline{)84}$ 4. $4\overline{)72}$

5. $7\overline{)84}$ 6. $6\overline{)78}$ 7. $8\overline{)96}$ 8. $5\overline{)85}$

9. $7\overline{)91}$ 10. $6\overline{)72}$ 11. $9\overline{)99}$ 12. $6\overline{)96}$ 13. $4\overline{)96}$

B

1. $3\overline{)48}$ 2. $4\overline{)68}$ 3. $6\overline{)72}$ 4. $4\overline{)56}$ 5. $5\overline{)65}$

6. $3\overline{)57}$ 7. $5\overline{)75}$ 8. $6\overline{)84}$ 9. $4\overline{)76}$ 10. $3\overline{)75}$

11. $7\overline{)84}$ 12. $8\overline{)96}$ 13. $5\overline{)95}$ 14. $3\overline{)87}$ 15. $7\overline{)91}$

Whole Numbers: Division

A

1. $2\overline{)20}$ 2. $3\overline{)60}$ 3. $4\overline{)60}$ 4. $2\overline{)40}$ 5. $2\overline{)30}$

6. $4\overline{)80}$ 7. $5\overline{)60}$ 8. $2\overline{)50}$ 9. $3\overline{)90}$ 10. $5\overline{)70}$

11. $6\overline{)60}$ 12. $2\overline{)70}$ 13. $5\overline{)80}$ 14. $9\overline{)90}$ 15. $6\overline{)90}$

- -

B

1. $3\overline{)30}$ 2. $2\overline{)40}$ 3. $4\overline{)40}$ 4. $2\overline{)30}$ 5. $3\overline{)60}$

6. $2\overline{)50}$ 7. $5\overline{)50}$ 8. $2\overline{)60}$ 9. $3\overline{)90}$ 10. $5\overline{)60}$

11. $4\overline{)60}$ 12. $7\overline{)70}$ 13. $4\overline{)80}$ 14. $5\overline{)90}$ 15. $2\overline{)70}$

Whole Numbers: Division

REMEMBER?
$\begin{array}{r} 1 \\ 2\overline{)224} \\ -\underline{2}{\downarrow} \end{array}$

A

1. $4\overline{)484}$ **2.** $5\overline{)555}$ **3.** $3\overline{)633}$

4. $6\overline{)666}$ **5.** $2\overline{)642}$ **6.** $4\overline{)448}$ **7.** $2\overline{)624}$

B

1. $2\overline{)242}$ **2.** $3\overline{)363}$ **3.** $6\overline{)666}$ **4.** $4\overline{)488}$

5. $3\overline{)636}$ **6.** $5\overline{)555}$ **7.** $2\overline{)662}$ **8.** $4\overline{)488}$

Name _____   Date _____

Whole Numbers: Division

REMEMBER?

$$\begin{array}{r} 1 \\ 2\overline{)\ 324} \\ -\ 2\downarrow \\ \hline 1 \end{array}$$

A

1. 4)568

2. 3)516

3. 6)726

4. 7)847

5. 4)648

6. 5)755

7. 2)584

- -

B

1. 3)576

2. 2)564

3. 4)688

4. 5)655

5. 2)586

6. 7)917

7. 4)524

8. 5)855

Whole Numbers: Division • Skill 3

Whole Numbers: Division

REMEMBER?
$\begin{array}{r} 10 \\ 3\overline{)306} \\ -\underline{3}\downarrow \end{array}$

A

1. $4\overline{)800}$ **2.** $2\overline{)400}$ **3.** $3\overline{)900}$

4. $5\overline{)505}$ **5.** $4\overline{)604}$ **6.** $2\overline{)500}$ **7.** $5\overline{)600}$

- -

B

1. $2\overline{)600}$ **2.** $3\overline{)300}$ **3.** $4\overline{)800}$ **4.** $9\overline{)900}$

5. $4\overline{)804}$ **6.** $7\overline{)707}$ **7.** $2\overline{)300}$ **8.** $5\overline{)700}$

Whole Numbers: Division

REMEMBER?

$$4 \overline{)288} \quad \begin{array}{r} 7 \\ \end{array}$$
$$-\underline{28}\downarrow$$

A

1. $4\overline{)288}$ **2.** $3\overline{)189}$ **3.** $2\overline{)184}$

4. $3\overline{)219}$ **5.** $6\overline{)246}$ **6.** $5\overline{)355}$ **7.** $5\overline{)305}$

B

1. $3\overline{)276}$ **2.** $2\overline{)164}$ **3.** $4\overline{)328}$ **4.** $3\overline{)156}$

5. $6\overline{)366}$ **6.** $5\overline{)405}$ **7.** $6\overline{)426}$ **8.** $5\overline{)455}$

Whole Numbers: Division

A

1. $2\overline{)112}$ **2.** $3\overline{)222}$ **3.** $3\overline{)261}$

4. $5\overline{)315}$ **5.** $5\overline{)245}$ **6.** $5\overline{)415}$

B

1. $3\overline{)282}$ **2.** $3\overline{)207}$ **3.** $4\overline{)296}$

4. $6\overline{)492}$ **5.** $6\overline{)516}$ **6.** $6\overline{)396}$

Whole Numbers: Division

REMEMBER?
$$\begin{array}{r} 1 \\ 4\overline{)720} \\ -\underline{4\downarrow} \\ 3 \end{array}$$

A

1. $3\overline{)780}$ 2. $5\overline{)750}$ 3. $4\overline{)424}$

4. $6\overline{)840}$ 5. $7\overline{)728}$ 6. $8\overline{)864}$ 7. $9\overline{)936}$

- -

B

1. $3\overline{)810}$ 2. $4\overline{)432}$ 3. $5\overline{)600}$ 4. $3\overline{)321}$

5. $6\overline{)780}$ 6. $9\overline{)909}$ 7. $8\overline{)960}$ 8. $7\overline{)840}$

Whole Numbers: Division

REMEMBER?

$$\begin{array}{r} 1{,}000 \\ 7{\overline{)7{,}000}} \\ -7{,}000 \\ \hline 0 \end{array}$$

A

1. $2{\overline{)6{,}000}}$ 2. $6{\overline{)7{,}800}}$ 3. $4{\overline{)9{,}600}}$

4. $5{\overline{)6{,}750}}$ 5. $6{\overline{)7{,}320}}$ 6. $4{\overline{)7{,}760}}$ 7. $3{\overline{)8{,}820}}$

- -

B

1. $5{\overline{)5{,}000}}$ 2. $3{\overline{)9{,}000}}$ 3. $6{\overline{)8{,}400}}$ 4. $4{\overline{)5{,}200}}$

5. $4{\overline{)6{,}920}}$ 6. $6{\overline{)7{,}920}}$ 7. $5{\overline{)7{,}250}}$ 8. $7{\overline{)8{,}540}}$

Whole Numbers: Division

A

1. $4\overline{)3,200}$ 2. $5\overline{)2,500}$ 3. $6\overline{)2,520}$ 4. $4\overline{)1,320}$

5. $6\overline{)4,368}$ 6. $7\overline{)5,796}$ 7. $5\overline{)4,785}$ 8. $4\overline{)3,616}$

- -

B

1. $6\overline{)3,600}$ 2. $7\overline{)4,200}$ 3. $5\overline{)2,650}$ 4. $4\overline{)1,760}$

5. $9\overline{)7,488}$ 6. $5\overline{)3,735}$ 7. $7\overline{)6,475}$ 8. $4\overline{)2,816}$

Whole Numbers: Division

REMEMBER?
$\begin{array}{r} 4 \\ 10\,\overline{)\,40} \\ -\ 40 \\ \hline 0 \end{array}$ $\begin{array}{r} 4 \\ \times\ 10 \\ \hline 40 \end{array}$

A

1. $40\,\overline{)\,80}$ **2.** $20\,\overline{)\,60}$ **3.** $10\,\overline{)\,70}$

4. $40\,\overline{)\,40}$ **5.** $20\,\overline{)\,80}$ **6.** $10\,\overline{)\,60}$ **7.** $20\,\overline{)\,20}$

- -

B

1. $30\,\overline{)\,60}$ **2.** $10\,\overline{)\,50}$ **3.** $20\,\overline{)\,20}$ **4.** $10\,\overline{)\,20}$

5. $10\,\overline{)\,40}$ **6.** $30\,\overline{)\,30}$ **7.** $40\,\overline{)\,80}$ **8.** $10\,\overline{)\,60}$

Whole Numbers: Division

REMEMBER?

$$12\overline{)48} \quad \begin{array}{r} 4 \\ \end{array}$$

$$\begin{array}{r} 4 \\ 12\overline{)48} \\ -\ 48 \\ \hline 0 \end{array} \quad \begin{array}{r} 4 \\ \times\ 12 \\ \hline 48 \end{array}$$

1. $11\overline{)55}$ **2.** $22\overline{)88}$ **3.** $21\overline{)63}$

4. $14\overline{)98}$ **5.** $21\overline{)84}$ **6.** $22\overline{)66}$ **7.** $13\overline{)39}$

8. $32\overline{)64}$ **9.** $42\overline{)84}$ **10.** $23\overline{)46}$ **11.** $31\overline{)62}$

12. $11\overline{)44}$ **13.** $34\overline{)68}$ **14.** $14\overline{)84}$ **15.** $19\overline{)57}$

Whole Numbers: Division

REMEMBER?
$\begin{array}{r} 2 \leftarrow 2 \\ 30\overline{)720} \quad \times 30 \\ -\underline{60} \quad \leftarrow 60 \end{array}$

A

1. $60\overline{)960}$ 2. $50\overline{)850}$ 3. $50\overline{)950}$

4. $70\overline{)840}$ 5. $60\overline{)840}$ 6. $10\overline{)890}$ 7. $30\overline{)600}$

- -

B

1. $20\overline{)640}$ 2. $40\overline{)680}$ 3. $30\overline{)990}$ 4. $50\overline{)900}$

5. $30\overline{)810}$ 6. $20\overline{)840}$ 7. $70\overline{)910}$ 8. $50\overline{)800}$

Whole Numbers: Division

REMEMBER?

$$\begin{array}{r} 4 \\ 18\overline{)738} \\ -\ 72 \\ \hline 18 \end{array} \quad \begin{array}{r} \leftarrow 4 \\ \times\ 18 \\ \leftarrow 72 \end{array}$$

A

1. $24\overline{)792}$ **2.** $12\overline{)312}$ **3.** $15\overline{)450}$

4. $24\overline{)864}$ **5.** $46\overline{)552}$ **6.** $32\overline{)832}$ **7.** $66\overline{)924}$

B

1. $12\overline{)744}$ **2.** $23\overline{)345}$ **3.** $13\overline{)962}$ **4.** $16\overline{)832}$

5. $18\overline{)882}$ **6.** $33\overline{)792}$ **7.** $46\overline{)966}$ **8.** $53\overline{)742}$

Whole Numbers: Division

A

1. $40 \overline{)4,920}$ 2. $30 \overline{)6,390}$ 3. $20 \overline{)6,400}$ 4. $60 \overline{)6,600}$

5. $50 \overline{)6,200}$ 6. $60 \overline{)8,520}$ 7. $80 \overline{)9,520}$ 8. $50 \overline{)6,650}$

B

1. $10 \overline{)1,560}$ 2. $20 \overline{)6,840}$ 3. $40 \overline{)8,840}$ 4. $10 \overline{)7,920}$

5. $40 \overline{)8,400}$ 6. $50 \overline{)5,500}$ 7. $20 \overline{)8,060}$ 8. $60 \overline{)7,140}$

Whole Numbers: Division

A

1. $36 \overline{)4{,}140}$ 2. $12 \overline{)2{,}148}$ 3. $14 \overline{)4{,}928}$ 4. $13 \overline{)7{,}254}$

5. $18 \overline{)8{,}874}$ 6. $12 \overline{)8{,}448}$ 7. $16 \overline{)8{,}864}$ 8. $12 \overline{)8{,}424}$

B

1. $19 \overline{)6{,}213}$ 2. $13 \overline{)8{,}632}$ 3. $18 \overline{)3{,}510}$ 4. $14 \overline{)6{,}608}$

5. $16 \overline{)5{,}552}$ 6. $16 \overline{)1{,}648}$ 7. $36 \overline{)4{,}464}$ 8. $23 \overline{)4{,}761}$

Whole Numbers: Division

SKILL 1

1. $4\overline{)28}$ **2.** $6\overline{)54}$ **3.** $9\overline{)72}$ **4.** $8\overline{)56}$ **5.** $7\overline{)63}$

SKILL 2

6. $4\overline{)84}$ **7.** $6\overline{)72}$ **8.** $4\overline{)72}$ **9.** $3\overline{)90}$ **10.** $3\overline{)48}$

SKILL 3

11. $5\overline{)305}$ **12.** $9\overline{)459}$ **13.** $7\overline{)448}$ **14.** $8\overline{)656}$ **15.** $6\overline{)546}$ ●

SKILL 4

16. $8\overline{)856}$ **17.** $5\overline{)550}$ **18.** $7\overline{)2,807}$ **19.** $9\overline{)8,199}$ **20.** $6\overline{)8,514}$

SKILL 5

21. $83\overline{)9,379}$ **22.** $42\overline{)5,082}$ **23.** $54\overline{)6,102}$ **24.** $38\overline{)8,018}$

Whole Numbers: Division

REMEMBER?
3R1
2)‾7‾ ↑
−6
1

A

1. $4\overline{)6}$ **2.** $5\overline{)7}$ **3.** $3\overline{)8}$ **4.** $6\overline{)9}$

5. $3\overline{)20}$ **6.** $3\overline{)23}$ **7.** $5\overline{)12}$ **8.** $3\overline{)29}$ **9.** $4\overline{)37}$

B

1. $3\overline{)8}$ **2.** $4\overline{)5}$ **3.** $5\overline{)8}$ **4.** $6\overline{)8}$ **5.** $4\overline{)7}$

6. $5\overline{)23}$ **7.** $3\overline{)10}$ **8.** $4\overline{)18}$ **9.** $2\overline{)11}$ **10.** $3\overline{)25}$

Whole Numbers: Division

REMEMBER?
157R1
3) 472

A

1. 7) 852

2. 5) 926

3. 4) 639

4. 6) 946

5. 4) 827

6. 7) 904

7. 3) 946

- -

B

1. 4) 654

2. 2) 359

3. 6) 928

4. 6) 788

5. 3) 538

6. 2) 963

7. 5) 742

8. 6) 629

Whole Numbers: Division

REMEMBER?
540R2
7) 3,782

A

1. 7) 2,860   2. 4) 2,650   3. 6) 2,960

4. 6) 2,133   5. 4) 3,501   6. 5) 1,353   7. 6) 4,924

- -

B

1. 6) 4,340   2. 7) 1,920   3. 3) 3,650   4. 6) 3,320

5. 7) 3,435   6. 4) 3,950   7. 5) 3,513   8. 3) 2,894

Whole Numbers: Division

REMEMBER?

$$30\overline{)67}$$ with $2R7$, -60, 7

1. $20\overline{)84}$

2. $30\overline{)75}$

3. $40\overline{)96}$

4. $30\overline{)51}$

5. $30\overline{)92}$

6. $40\overline{)59}$

7. $50\overline{)67}$

8. $47\overline{)97}$

9. $13\overline{)77}$

10. $23\overline{)98}$

11. $52\overline{)63}$

12. $17\overline{)82}$

13. $36\overline{)73}$

14. $42\overline{)83}$

15. $19\overline{)85}$

Whole Numbers: Division

A

1. $30 \overline{) 208}$ **2.** $40 \overline{) 161}$ **3.** $50 \overline{) 252}$ **4.** $40 \overline{) 209}$

5. $32 \overline{) 187}$ **6.** $41 \overline{) 147}$ **7.** $32 \overline{) 161}$ **8.** $51 \overline{) 262}$

B

1. $50 \overline{) 302}$ **2.** $40 \overline{) 283}$ **3.** $30 \overline{) 154}$ **4.** $60 \overline{) 243}$

5. $51 \overline{) 428}$ **6.** $42 \overline{) 379}$ **7.** $34 \overline{) 243}$ **8.** $21 \overline{) 183}$

Whole Numbers: Division

A

1. $13 \overline{)1,971}$ 2. $34 \overline{)7,044}$ 3. $29 \overline{)9,508}$ 4. $26 \overline{)4,174}$

5. $66 \overline{)7,031}$ 6. $75 \overline{)9,413}$ 7. $29 \overline{)9,223}$ 8. $53 \overline{)7,284}$

B

1. $26 \overline{)5,864}$ 2. $36 \overline{)9,047}$ 3. $54 \overline{)8,146}$ 4. $23 \overline{)7,821}$

5. $18 \overline{)3,049}$ 6. $29 \overline{)9,361}$ 7. $46 \overline{)7,493}$ 8. $65 \overline{)8,004}$

Whole Numbers: Division

A

REMEMBER?

$$230\overline{)993} \quad \begin{array}{r} 4R73 \\ -920 \\ \hline 73 \end{array}$$

1. $14\overline{)741}$ **2.** $31\overline{)817}$ **3.** $25\overline{)864}$

4. $16\overline{)4{,}901}$ **5.** $21\overline{)8{,}734}$ **6.** $12\overline{)8{,}058}$ **7.** $32\overline{)6{,}973}$

- -

B

1. $21\overline{)430}$ **2.** $15\overline{)601}$ **3.** $31\overline{)943}$ **4.** $41\overline{)832}$

5. $53\overline{)7{,}092}$ **6.** $43\overline{)9{,}372}$ **7.** $31\overline{)7{,}455}$ **8.** $62\overline{)7{,}573}$

Whole Numbers: Division

REMEMBER?
$2R69$
$207\overline{)483}$

A

1. $321\overline{)736}$ **2.** $840\overline{)867}$

3. $307\overline{)7,960}$ **4.** $521\overline{)6,652}$ **5.** $846\overline{)9,423}$

- -

B

1. $853\overline{)938}$ **2.** $626\overline{)963}$ **3.** $509\overline{)710}$ **4.** $642\overline{)837}$

5. $581\overline{)5,921}$ **6.** $702\overline{)8,503}$ **7.** $462\overline{)7,401}$

Whole Numbers: Division

REMEMBER?
 295R9
$38 \overline{)\ 11,219}$

A

1. $38 \overline{)\ 11,224}$

2. $58 \overline{)\ 12,377}$

3. $25 \overline{)\ 64,213}$

4. $59 \overline{)\ 62,909}$

5. $43 \overline{)\ 78,840}$

B

1. $89 \overline{)\ 84,020}$

2. $24 \overline{)\ 12,397}$

3. $73 \overline{)\ 18,347}$

4. $37 \overline{)\ 25,018}$

5. $16 \overline{)\ 45,662}$

6. $28 \overline{)\ 32,605}$

Whole Numbers: Division

1. 329) 18,425

2. 637) 59,187

3. 199) 16,461

4. 207) 35,820

5. 545) 23,634

6. 538) 65,363

7. 290) 17,340

8. 836) 59,735

9. 167) 15,998

10. 257) 51,501

11. 306) 20,606

12. 801) 50,071

Whole Numbers: Division

1. 293) 674,330   **2.** 182) 374,310   **3.** 251) 767,507

4. 135) 467,702   **5.** 210) 114,231   **6.** 778) 843,454

7. 395) 400,008   **8.** 421) 707,050   **9.** 512) 541,005

10. 801) 950,412   **11.** 703) 852,002   **12.** 306) 800,791

Whole Numbers: Division

REMEMBER?
$7\frac{2}{6}$
$6\overline{)44}$
-42
2

A

Write all remainders as fractions.

1. $9\overline{)75}$ **2.** $7\overline{)78}$ **3.** $8\overline{)84}$ **4.** $3\overline{)43}$

5. $8\overline{)139}$ **6.** $5\overline{)146}$ **7.** $7\overline{)961}$ **8.** $6\overline{)795}$ **9.** $9\overline{)977}$

- -

B

Write all remainders as fractions.

1. $6\overline{)34}$ **2.** $9\overline{)65}$ **3.** $7\overline{)64}$ **4.** $8\overline{)62}$ **5.** $3\overline{)53}$

6. $8\overline{)137}$ **7.** $5\overline{)143}$ **8.** $7\overline{)862}$ **9.** $6\overline{)784}$ **10.** $9\overline{)874}$

Whole Numbers: Division

REMEMBER?
$4\frac{11}{22}$
$22\overline{)99}$
-88
11

A

Write all remainders as fractions.

1. $33\overline{)86}$ **2.** $43\overline{)54}$ **3.** $27\overline{)86}$ **4.** $18\overline{)94}$

5. $46\overline{)702}$ **6.** $86\overline{)901}$ **7.** $18\overline{)503}$ **8.** $85\overline{)994}$

B

Write all remainders as fractions.

1. $24\overline{)83}$ **2.** $35\overline{)76}$ **3.** $44\overline{)63}$ **4.** $28\overline{)73}$ **5.** $19\overline{)85}$

6. $47\overline{)704}$ **7.** $85\overline{)903}$ **8.** $17\overline{)702}$ **9.** $84\overline{)875}$

Whole Numbers: Division

A

Write all remainders as fractions.

1. $408\overline{)567}$ 2. $608\overline{)926}$ 3. $926\overline{)987}$ 4. $444\overline{)995}$

5. $392\overline{)2{,}877}$ 6. $545\overline{)3{,}897}$ 7. $209\overline{)1{,}453}$ 8. $632\overline{)3{,}206}$

B

Write all remainders as fractions.

1. $452\overline{)893}$ 2. $232\overline{)865}$ 3. $329\overline{)997}$ 4. $326\overline{)447}$

5. $167\overline{)6{,}703}$ 6. $267\overline{)2{,}976}$ 7. $360\overline{)8{,}432}$ 8. $109\overline{)2{,}984}$

Whole Numbers: Division

REMEMBER?

$$8 \overline{)\begin{array}{c} 8.87 \\ 71.00 \end{array}}$$

A

Write all answers in decimal form.
Round to the nearest hundredth.

1. $3 \overline{)19}$ **2.** $5 \overline{)18}$ **3.** $6 \overline{)39}$

4. $4 \overline{)146}$ **5.** $9 \overline{)794}$ **6.** $9 \overline{)119}$ **7.** $5 \overline{)216}$

B

Write all answers in decimal form.
Round to the nearest hundredth.

1. $5 \overline{)16}$ **2.** $3 \overline{)22}$ **3.** $5 \overline{)23}$ **4.** $6 \overline{)47}$

5. $4 \overline{)135}$ **6.** $9 \overline{)682}$ **7.** $9 \overline{)121}$ **8.** $5 \overline{)217}$

Whole Numbers: Division

REMEMBER?
1.555
27) 42.000

A

Write all answers in decimal form.
Round to the nearest hundredth.

1. 16) 92   **2.** 27) 42   **3.** 43) 95

4. 23) 861   **5.** 37) 743   **6.** 54) 964   **7.** 68) 801

●

- -

B

Write all answers in decimal form.
Round to the nearest hundredth.

1. 49) 77   **2.** 32) 80   **3.** 68) 74   **4.** 91) 96

5. 78) 942   **6.** 81) 977   **7.** 37) 742   **8.** 59) 628

●

Whole Numbers: Division

REMEMBER?

$$29\overline{)342.000}^{11.793}$$

Rounded
11.79

Write all answers in decimal form.
Round to the nearest hundredth.

1. $43\overline{)676}$ **2.** $61\overline{)712}$ **3.** $74\overline{)268}$

4. $24\overline{)860}$ **5.** $55\overline{)963}$ **6.** $68\overline{)900}$ **7.** $45\overline{)470}$

8. $71\overline{)8,014}$ **9.** $65\overline{)7,484}$ **10.** $26\overline{)4,213}$ **11.** $37\overline{)9,446}$

12. $35\overline{)9,352}$ **13.** $64\overline{)7,482}$ **14.** $86\overline{)9,021}$ **15.** $70\overline{)7,004}$

Whole Numbers: Division

SKILL 6

1. $62 \overline{)4{,}263}$ **2.** $53 \overline{)6{,}392}$ **3.** $41 \overline{)9{,}256}$ **4.** $32 \overline{)6{,}744}$

SKILL 7

5. $257 \overline{)51{,}510}$ **6.** $701 \overline{)40{,}008}$ **7.** $167 \overline{)14{,}986}$

SKILL 8

Write all remainders as fractions.

8. $165 \overline{)6{,}704}$ **9.** $268 \overline{)2{,}975}$ **10.** $370 \overline{)8{,}433}$

SKILL 9

Write all answers in decimal form.
Round to the nearest hundredth.

11. $64 \overline{)7{,}484}$ **12.** $74 \overline{)1{,}708}$ **13.** $86 \overline{)9{,}032}$ **14.** $69 \overline{)4{,}203}$

Whole Numbers: Division

SKILL 1

1. $5 \overline{)45}$ **2.** $7 \overline{)56}$ **3.** $4 \overline{)32}$ **4.** $6 \overline{)48}$ **5.** $9 \overline{)81}$

SKILL 2

6. $3 \overline{)36}$ **7.** $7 \overline{)91}$ **8.** $4 \overline{)56}$ **9.** $5 \overline{)60}$ **10.** $6 \overline{)84}$

SKILL 3

11. $7 \overline{)217}$ **12.** $8 \overline{)648}$ **13.** $5 \overline{)375}$ **14.** $6 \overline{)390}$ **15.** $9 \overline{)828}$

SKILL 4

16. $6 \overline{)882}$ **17.** $4 \overline{)660}$ **18.** $8 \overline{)7,208}$ **19.** $5 \overline{)7,550}$

SKILL 5

20. $40 \overline{)80}$ **21.** $50 \overline{)950}$ **22.** $42 \overline{)126}$ **23.** $82 \overline{)7,790}$

Whole Numbers: Division

SKILL 6

24. $4\overline{)39}$ **25.** $8\overline{)965}$ **26.** $5\overline{)4,517}$ **27.** $17\overline{)60}$ **28.** $54\overline{)433}$

SKILL 7

29. $17\overline{)5,209}$ **30.** $408\overline{)8,737}$ **31.** $81\overline{)34,136}$ **32.** $189\overline{)16,350}$

SKILL 8

Write all remainders as fractions.

33. $5\overline{)757}$ **34.** $17\overline{)88}$ **35.** $412\overline{)2,497}$ **36.** $325\overline{)1,475}$

SKILL 9

Write all answers in decimal form.
Round to the nearest hundredth.

37. $4\overline{)171}$ **38.** $26\overline{)495}$ **39.** $64\overline{)7,482}$ **40.** $69\overline{)4,102}$

STUDENT PROGRESS CHART

Strand 4: Whole Numbers: Division

Inventory

Score:_____ of 9

Skill 1

Page 1:_____ of 38
Page 2:_____ of 39
Page 3:_____ of 38
Page 4:_____ of 40
Page 5:_____ of 50
Page 6:_____ of 50

Skill 2

Page 1:_____ of 28
Page 2:_____ of 28
Page 3:_____ of 30

Skill 3

Page 1:_____ of 15
Page 2:_____ of 15
Page 3:_____ of 15
Page 4:_____ of 15
Page 5:_____ of 12

Skill 4

Page 1:_____ of 15
Page 2:_____ of 15
Page 3:_____ of 16

Skill 5

Page 1:_____ of 15
Page 2:_____ of 15
Page 3:_____ of 15
Page 4:_____ of 15
Page 5:_____ of 16
Page 6:_____ of 16
Review 1–5:_____ of 24

Skill 6

Page 1:_____ of 19
Page 2:_____ of 15
Page 3:_____ of 15
Page 4:_____ of 15
Page 5:_____ of 16
Page 6:_____ of 16

Skill 7

Page 1:_____ of 15
Page 2:_____ of 12
Page 3:_____ of 11
Page 4:_____ of 12
Page 5:_____ of 12

Skill 8

Page 1:_____ of 19
Page 2:_____ of 17
Page 3:_____ of 16

Skill 9

Page 1:_____ of 15
Page 2:_____ of 15
Page 3:_____ of 15
Review 6–9:_____ of 14
Cumulative
   Review: _____ of 40